Third Edition

90% Of Helping Is Just Showing Up!

JAMES R. KOK

The discussion suggestions that accompany each chapter were prepared by Craig Bourne.

90% of Helping Is Just Showing Up!, © 1996, 2006 (Second Edition) by Faith Alive Christian Resources, 2850 Kalamazoo Ave. SE, Grand Rapids, MI 49560, 2014 (Third Edition) by Care and Kindness Ministries. 10073 Valley View Street, #429, Cypress, California 90630.

ISBN-13: 978-1496113795
ISBN-10: 1496113799
90% Of Helping Is Just Showing Up!
©2014 by James R. Kok.

Published by Care and Kindness Ministries
10073 Valley View Street, #429
Cypress, California 90630

CONTENTS

Introduction 7

1. What People Really Need 9
   Give them intimacy, not answers

2. It Takes Courage To Show Up 15
   90% of helping is just showing up

3. Speak Up About What You Feel And Think....................21
   You have something everybody needs

4. Reasonable Questions Can Hurt....................................27
   Was he wearing a helmet?

5. Act Friendly Anyway 31
   How to increase global warming

6. You Need To Take A Closer Look...............................37
   Everything looks different close-up

7. Speedy Escapes Deprive Us Of Vital Lessons.................... 43
   The joy and sorrow of changing a light bulb

8. Every Person Is A Potential Healer 49
   How ordinary people helped save a life

9. The Player And The Umpire See The Game Differently............55
   Are you an umpire or a player

10. Wake-Up Calls Irritate, but Enlighten, Too....................61
    A mild earthquake is good for the soul

11. Generous Giving Has Limitations..67
    Giving is great, but receiving is essential, too

12. Resurrection Power Works Wonders Every Day............................73
    After a hurricane, search for flowers

13. There Is A Time To Give — And Ask No Questions 79
    A banquet in West Hollywood

14. If Jesus Were My Teacher...85

INTRODUCTION

I want to be a caring person. I want to help others feel they are cared for. From the depth of my being, I have learned that caring is an art form, and every day I seek to share the discoveries of my journey—being there and caring by doing.

Caring is not a feeling. Strong feelings or deep concerns for another person may be called caring, but until those feelings or concerns trigger constructive action on the other's behalf, they are only interesting emotions.

Caring is best understood by looking at God. Until God became human, we could not knowingly experience his love. Incarnation was essential. The Word had to become flesh—an audiovisual, tactile message we could understand.

Christ's people continue to live by this model. They turn feelings into concrete, observable, practical expressions of love. Awareness of need is turned into positive help. That's caring!

Feelings are a gift from God. We can respect, value, and listen to them. But they are intended to move us to do something. They have little worth unless they ignite a plan, which will then be followed by deeds that improve the world—by helping to correct or modify the pain or injustice in another's life, for example.

All the hurt we feel when we learn of a friend's serious illness does not make us caring people. My deep mental anguish over the plight of someone cut by unemployment does not prove I am a caring person. When it comes to caring, having strong—even agonizing—sympathy means little. Talking gravely, too, proves nothing. Only action counts as sympathy (empathy).

Action may be prayer, an understanding word, a personal visit, a phone call, or a card (always with a handwritten note). It may be attendance at a graduation, wedding, funeral, or a farewell open house. Being there is caring.

There are endless practical ways to care for others when tough times occur. Wendy Bergen, a woman struggling with cancer, wrote down some of her ideas. They range from very concrete ways of helping—bringing food or offering to baby-sit—to the more abstract ways of showing concern—allowing a person to feel sad, touching them, telling them how great they look, and sharing humor. Bergen's ideas suggest how resourcefulness can produce especially helpful acts of caring.

Turning our feelings into deeds models Christ's incarnation—the Word becoming flesh.

Chapter 1

What People Really Need

Most people want to be helpful. They will try to aid and assist friends in need in a variety of practical and resourceful ways. Caring colleagues generously support each other through many creative, self-denying acts and gifts.

But one mode of helping easily gets overlooked in the human rush to make things better for fallen comrades. Call it "just being there" or "walking with" or "intimacy." Often this is the most vital ingredient in any recipe for restoring a broken heart or a shattered spirit.

Give them intimacy, not answers

People need intimacy, not answers—that is what we must remember when we are trying to comfort someone who is hurting. Unfortunately the typical response to another's distress is to try to give answers. Our tongues swing into high speed, and we overflow with glib sayings and spiritual moralisms. Few of our words help; some even irritate or distance us from the people we are trying to help.

Some years ago in a small group setting I spoke candidly about my dismay over the devastating illness of a dear friend. Needing comfort, I received instead a lecture on current cancer treatments and an assurance that "a miracle can always happen, you know." I politely thanked the lecturer for his concern, but his comments weren't helpful to me.

The Way of the Wolf by Martin Bell contains a wonderful story titled "The Porcupine Whose Name Didn't Matter." For obvious reasons the porcupine was a misfit in society and had no friends. But one day he stumbled upon a raccoon who had been shot and was near death. The porcupine remained with the raccoon and heard its sad story. Then both fell silent. After a while the raccoon asked, "Are you still there?"

"Yes," replied the porcupine, "I'm still here. I was just wondering what to do now."

"Oh, you don't have to do anything!" said the dying raccoon. "Honestly, I mean that. Just stay with me for a little while. Just be there. Don't go away, please. I'm afraid. You won't go away, will you?"

Perhaps the reason that the simple gift of intimacy is so difficult to give is that it is best given with silence. However, when we are silent in the face of suffering, we run headlong into a terrible feeling of helplessness. If we talk or actively assist, we feel helpful; just "being there" confronts us with our own weakness and dependency.

To bring comfort, we must learn to be comfortable with this feeling of helplessness. Job's comforters did well when they sat with him in silence. Then their anxiety got the best of them, and endless stupidities flowed from their mouths.

The apostle Paul advises us to "weep with those who weep." Paul realized that people who are hurting are often helped more by a kindred spirit shedding tears of empathy than by advice and counsel. Proverbs 25 : 20 (NRSV) says, "He who sings songs to a heavy heart is like one who takes off a garment on a cold day, and like vinegar on a wound."

In *The Book of the Dun Cow* by Walter Wangerin, Jr., we learn of the healing power of presence, of "being there," when the Dun Cow comes to comfort the injured and grieving Chanticleer, the regal rooster:

> She put her soft nose against him, to nudge him into a more peaceful position. Gently she arranged his head so that he might clearly see her. Her sweet breath went into his nostrils. . . . The Dun Cow took a single step back from the rooster then and looked at him. . . . Her eyes were liquid with compassion—deep, deep, as the earth is deep. Her brow knew his suffering and knew besides that, worlds more. But the goodness was that, though this wide brow knew so much, yet it bent over his pain alone and creased with it.

> Chanticleer watched his own desolation appear in the eyes of the Cow, then sink so deeply into them that she shuddered. Her eyes pooled as she looked at him. The tears rose and spilled over. . . . He watched—felt—the miracle take place. Nothing changed: The clouds would not be removed, nor his sons returned, nor his knowledge plenished. But there was this: his grief had become her grief, his sorrow her own. And though he grieved not one bit less for that, yet his heart made room for her, for her will and wisdom, and he bore the sorrow better.

The Dun Cow represents God's presence, from whom we draw all healing. But in this spirit-renewing episode, we also are reminded of the blessing our presence can be to others.

Sometimes we act as if the best things God has given us are words, information, and answers. In reality, God's best gift may well be his caring presence amid our confusion and struggles. Certainly the best gift we can give anyone is our presence: our crying, hugging, waiting, listening, smiling, and sharing.

If you ask weak, ailing, or aged persons what Scripture they would like to hear, many of them will request Psalm 23. Why? Because when we are in need, we want a relationship, not an explanation. Psalm 23 provides a comforting picture of the companionship, support, and presence of the good shepherd. When we read the psalm, we feel the Lord walking by our side.

The biggest challenge for many of us is to learn to eliminate our need to answer and fix, to straighten others out, to give them advice. Once we conquer this tendency, we can find the quiet strength to walk with others through their dark valleys. A current saying captures that thought well: "I do not care how much you know until I know how much you care."

Reflections

1. *"People need intimacy, not answers."* Describe a time when you found yourself offering intimacy first, even before asking the questions that were calling for answers in your mind.

    Who is there, right now, to whom you might reach out in some way? What can you, or will you do?

2. *"I'm still here. I was just wondering what to do now."* Can you put yourself into the scene with the raccoon and the porcupine? Describe the feelings of awkwardness and helplessness of the porcupine.

3. *"Perhaps the reason that the simple gift of intimacy is so difficult to give is that it is best given with silence."* What makes it hard to reach out and "show up" in loving kindness to someone?

4. *"Just stay with me for a little while. Just be there. Don't go away, please."* What similar words has someone said to you that remind you of the words of the raccoon?

5. *"Oh, you don't have to do anything!' said the dying raccoon."* Share a memory of a time when you needed someone to 'walk with you'. Tell about how it turned out.

6. *"Job's comforters did well when they sat with him in silence. Then their anxiety got the best of them, and endless stupidities flowed from their mouths."* Weren't the reactions of the group of Job's comforters the way most people respond? What do you think you would have done or said?

7. *"Chanticleer watched his own desolation appear in the eyes of the Cow, then sink so deeply into them that she shuddered. Her eyes pooled as she looked at him. The tears rose and spilled over."* Have you wrestled with understanding the difference between empathy and sympathy? Explain how the Dun Cow embodies being truly empathetic.

8. *"The biggest challenge for many of us is to learn to eliminate our need to answer and fix, to straighten others out, to give them advice."* Do you now recognize more clearly your own tendency to want to 'fix' a sorrowful or stressful situation for someone? Describe one such instance.

9. *"When we read the psalm, we feel the Lord walking by our side."* What feelings do you experience when you give loving-kindness to someone?

Chapter 2

It Takes Courage To Show Up

Many Christians yearn to put their lives on the line for the Lord and lament the lack of opportunities to do so in our modern society. Meanwhile wonderful challenges that surround them slip by unnoticed or are wrongly assessed.

A new frontier of Christian service beckons. It is the call of the weak and wounded for people who will share their distress and help lift their pressing burdens. Many people shrink from this daunting cry, believing themselves to be inadequate or ill-equipped. To these self-discounting saints the Lord whispers, "Just show up; I'll do the rest."

90% of helping is just showing up

Tragic circumstances set people apart. When disaster strikes or a loved one dies, a wall goes up, separating these devastated folks from others.

On Christmas morning, 1990, a fire ravaged the home of neighbors a few houses from ours. Crowds quickly gathered to watch the fire department fight the stubborn blaze. I noticed among the onlookers a barefooted, barebacked man sitting alone on the curb. His face and chest looked severely sunburned. I figured he was the home owner.

It did not seem right to leave him sitting there all alone, but I thought, "What can I say to him?" I couldn't think of anything very helpful. Still I knew I had to go up to him.

Me: "Did everyone get out all right?"

He: "Yes."

Me: "Do you have a place to stay?"

He: "Yes, my mother-in-law lives in South Gate."

Me: "Did you get burned?"

He: "Yes, I was on the roof with the hose trying to put it out while waiting for the blankety-blank fire trucks to get here."

Finally, another person, apparently a relative, came up and sat beside him. I seized the opportunity to escape, feeling as if I had intruded into his private space. I also felt that I had done the right thing, however clumsily.

"Sorry, my friend," I said in parting.

"Thanks," he replied, and it seemed genuine.

It is easy to snap jumper cables onto a neighbor's dead battery and start her car. Handing a few dollars to a cashless friend or a homeless panhandler can feel good too. Repairing an older person's broken door latch is simple, effective, and gratifying.

But helping with the irreversible is something quite different. Folks fade in the face of that which is unfixable. And perhaps they should—at least when it comes to thinking there are magic formulas to solve such plights. Only fools rush in with words, advice, ideas, and answers—inappropriate salve for open wounds.

It is one thing to be struck dumb by death or destruction, to be tongue-tied when wishing to say something beneficial. Such speechlessness is appropriate. It is another matter to stay away, to avoid, to merely be a spectator around the bent, battered, and broken.

The mother of a Down's syndrome child, for example, may observe how other mothers and their children sneak glances at them as they shop the supermarket aisles. She hears their whispers. No oohing and aahing over her baby. Just silence and distance.

Death and death-like circumstances severely tax our human need to control. The birth of a developmentally disabled infant, rape, robbery, loss of something valued, death, child abuse—all of these must be accepted as senseless tragedies that cannot be undone. And all of them leave us feeling helpless.

Nearly twenty years ago a middle-aged man, an elder in his church, told me that his best friend was dying of cancer. He then said something that has haunted me ever since: "I can't go to see him. It just disturbs me too much." Here was a spiritual leader allowing his friend to die without his support because he felt so awful in the dying man's presence.

This elder was not unusual. Those who wish to do better at sharing the private pain of others will frequently beg off because they don't know what to say to the hurting person. What they don't realize is that such inadequate feelings may be their best credentials. Over and over again I assure people that just showing up is 90 percent of the help they can offer. I advise them to avoid pat answers but assure them that even pat answers will be forgiven—because they cared enough to call.

We Christians are called to cross the valley and enter the space where we feel helpless and speechless. The Lord entreats us to silence our inner screams of terror over feeling dumb and empty-handed and to say something simple like "Hello" or "I love you." Christ exhorts us to override our own tearfulness, sadness, and pity, and to approach what we wish mightily to escape. When we do so, we often find that something good happens: the wall comes down; we have entered another's pain.

Almost every day I, as a pastor, have to walk into these awesome circumstances. I have never felt as if I've become good at dealing with them or have achieved perfect ease. And even though I enter these valleys often and my presence frequently yields rewarding results, I have not become comfortable with them. Like you, I try to find ways to avoid that fearful task of once again entering another's private, personal world of pain and disappointment. Because it is my professional responsibility, however, I rarely find an exit.

The Christian community should hold the franchise on Christlike burden-bearing, a task universally avoided. Jesus died for us. We die for others when we vacate our comfort zones, the places where we are in control, and stand closer to the heartbroken. We may feel helpless, weak, and tongue-tied, but we can know that we are partners in doing what is right.

Reflections

1. *"Helping with the irreversible is something quite different."* Are you more likely to try to say something beneficial, or to stay away and avoid close involvement? Why do you think you tend to do that?

2. *"I can't go to see him. It just disturbs me too much."* Why is 'just showing up' so important?

3. *"It is one thing to be struck dumb by death or destruction, to be tongue-tied when wishing to say something beneficial."* What might keep you from making a phone call to a recently "widowed" man or woman?

4. *"We may feel helpless, weak, and tongue-tied, but we can know that we are partners in doing what is right."* Loving-kindness makes people feel better. Does the giver get as much as the receiver? Why? Why not?

5. *"We die for others when we vacate our comfort zones."* What does this statement mean to you? What do you think of the idea that visiting a lonely or injured person is like Jesus dying for us?

6. *"Avoid pat answers."* When someone tells you, 'I am so awfully sad', what would be a meaningful response?

Chapter 3

Speak Up About What You Feel And Think

Unspoken praise, unuttered appreciation, unused compliments bounce around inside most of us. Sometimes they leak out in miserly fashion. Occasionally they overflow rapturously. Mostly they stack up unsaid and slip away, blessing no one.

Why is it that compliments are so hard to give away? We feel them, think them, know how they bless people. Still we find it so difficult to say them.

You have something everybody needs

"Pastor," said the young man warmly as he exited the church, "that was a very special sermon. Why, it was like water to a drowning man."

A fine speaker was thanked with these words: "We are not unhappy that we invited you."

Most of us do not easily or frequently pay good, clear compliments. In fact, a majority of churchgoers never speak a single compliment to a pastor in their entire lives. It's not that they're being selective; they don't give compliments to anybody.

Many people tend to view compliments as unnecessary luxuries. There is no point in giving them and no discomfort over not receiving them, say these rugged individualists. That's just the way life is.

But everybody needs encouraging words. A spirit-lifting sentence, properly placed, sets off a chain reaction of goodwill that goes on and on. It is one of the simplest ways to make this world a better place. Like a mega dose of vitamins in a malnourished body, compliments replenish depleted self-confidence. And the wonderful thing about it is that anybody can be a part of this ministry of kindness. Starved egos feast hungrily on any morsels offered, no matter who gives them.

At times Christians look wistfully at missionaries and Bible translators who are diligently slaving in distant lands. They lament that they are just pew-sitting believers. They feel that they add little to the kingdom of God besides their tithes and offerings.

Meanwhile they live and work among dozens of famished folks, who long for a soul-nourishing snack from the believers' overloaded storehouse of blessings. Vital kingdom building happens when we speak complimentary sentences to those around us. This is a mission every Christian can participate in, confident of doing the Lord's work. A good word is a word from God.

In my first year as an ordained minister, I worked as a chaplain

in a large state hospital in New York state. Thousands of patients resided there, most with serious mental illness. Some staggered and groaned with brain damage or other mental impairment.

As a fledgling pastor, I worried about preaching to those people. But Sunday after Sunday I delivered the gospel to this amazing crowd.

After a few weeks, it dawned on me that following the service, the same man always greeted me with a handshake and the mumbled words, "Good sermon." I soon noticed that I eagerly anticipated seeing him each Sunday because his barely audible words clearly buoyed my sagging confidence.

Later I learned that Ernie was mentally impaired, not mentally ill. I had a sneaking suspicion he didn't truly know a good sermon from a bad one. But it didn't matter. Ernie, with an IQ of 53, had become a very important cheerleader for me.

Many years ago, I received a complimentary letter from a man I did not know. He liked something I had written. It was the first bold, blatant, outrageous pat on the back I had ever received, outside of athletics. The man's name was Maurice Te Paske, and I will never forget him. I can close my eyes and see the paper and his lavish signature to this day. He blessed me profoundly by his simple, thoughtful words of appreciation.

Maurice knew something every Christian must take to heart: people need something from every one of us. Maurice starred. Others stumble trying.

In the hearts of everyone lie stacks of thoughts and feelings of appreciation and admiration for others. Mostly they stay inside, unexpressed. In addition to our spontaneous, unspoken reactions are a lot more encouraging words, easily conjured up, through a little reflection about the good and faithful deeds of those around us. About these, God's people must speak up!

The writer of Hebrews calls on his readers to "encourage each other every day." Because encouraged people feel loved, they work better and stay healthier. They become wealthy in spirit and mind. They themselves then overflow with good words.

Unfortunately, some intended compliments contain unintended putdowns. Many of us have been on the receiving end of well-meaning gifts like "You have really improved." What that really means is "You were pretty bad before, but are not so bad now." Even the words "You really look nice today" can be perceived as a two-edged commentary.

Most people get uneasy about compliments. They haven't learned how to respond to a positive word with a simple reply of "Thank you, I needed that." Because a majority of encouraging words have to hit moving targets, shooting them out clearly and briefly works best.

We must always keep in mind that it is the Spirit of God who generates compliments, encouraging words, and appreciation. We serve as the appointed conduits of the Spirit's whisperings, charged with depositing these gifts on needy candidates all around us.

Reflections

1. *"Many people tend to view compliments as unnecessary luxuries."* Why do you think this statement is true? Why is it that compliments are so hard to give away?

2. *"A good word is a word from God."* What are your thoughts about these words?

3. *"Vital kingdom building happens when we speak complimentary sentences to those around us."* Why does the giving of a compliment have such a great impact, even to being called 'kingdom building'?

4. *"Compliments replenish depleted self-confidence."* To whom could you make a call today, and give an appreciative word?

5. *"Most people haven't learned how to respond to a positive word with a simple reply of 'Thank you, I needed that.'"* What do you say in response to someone's compliment? What kind of responses do you get from others when you compliment them?

6. *"Most people get uneasy about compliments."* How do you act and feel when your compliment is laughed at, or ignored?

7. *"We serve as the appointed conduits of the Spirit's whisperings."* How do you think such a simple thing as a compliment is connected with the Holy Spirit?

Chapter 4

Reasonable Questions Can Hurt

Smart people sidestep pain. Personal experience teaches us early in life that pain hurts and should be avoided.

Some people learn effective pain-evasion tactics too well. These folks become neatly insulated even from the sorrow and anguish of those near them for whom they sincerely want to care.

One technique people often use to keep pain at a distance is questioning—especially the kind that focuses on facts and slips directly toward fault-finding. Kindly people, blind to their habits and unreflective about their words, often wing arrows of blame into already wounded hearts through seemingly innocuous inquiries.

Was he wearing a helmet?

She came to the grief group because of the death of her son. A "biker," or motorcyclist, he had been killed while challenging the mountain curves on the Angeles Crest Highway, a death-defying pastime of many of his colleagues on two wheels.

One by one the group members told their stories. Most of them had lost spouses, one a mother. All had come to the group to find support for the pain of their losses. When the woman's turn came, she simply and tearfully said, "My only son was killed in a motorcycling accident."

The first question she was asked by another mourner was totally expected and yet disturbingly inappropriate—predictable, but so lacking in compassion from a fellow sufferer that it was shocking: "Was he wearing a helmet?" Surely an uncaring question in the face of such heartbreak.

A colleague's young son died recently of AIDS. Sharing this tragedy with friends, I immediately encountered their queries: "Was he gay?" When other tragedies strike, people ask questions of the same ilk: "Was she wearing a seatbelt?" (auto accident); "Was she a smoker?" (lung cancer); "Was he on drugs?" (teen suicide).

What value does this information have to the inquirer? When you are face-to-face with grieving people, what difference does it make if he was wearing a helmet or a seatbelt, if she was a smoker or was gay? When a life is extinguished, certain officials may need to note these details, but caring folks seem to need to know as well.

The most innocent explanation may be that human beings have a compulsion to complete the picture. Asking these questions enables them to put together a scenario with relevant pieces in place before empathizing with the pain.

Another possibility, less innocuous, is that we are congenital blamers. We are driven to diagnose faults, to find causes, to point out the guilty party or the behavior involved. We probe relentlessly for facts and smugly pass judgment.

Although both of these explanations are partially accurate, another reason for these ill-conceived questions makes even greater sense: such queries spring up as a means to avoid pain, to sidestep blunt heartache. A prime way to care less is to find a way to blame the victim. Perhaps that is why the death of a child is so awful. We can't distance ourselves by finding a way in which the child brought the tragedy on himself.

Subliminally, we soften harsh circumstances by the following kind of thinking: "If he was stupid enough to be riding without a helmet; if he was foolhardy enough to ignore seatbelt laws; if she was crazy enough to smoke cigarettes . . . then I don't have to get quite so disturbed about this death."

The terrible AIDS plague fits this notion exactly. In the minds and hearts of the non-homosexual majority (and on their lips as well) is the callous assessment "They brought it on themselves; why should we get all upset about it?"

This is a hazardous posture to assume. Stress, cigarettes, alcohol, eating habits, lifestyles, neglect, corporately caused genetic damage, environmental hazards, sloth, competitiveness, bad habits, and anger cause or exacerbate most life-threatening conditions. If we reserve compassion for the truly innocent, few are going to be worthy.

According to this notion, God must rest in a pretty comfortable position. From God's viewpoint, we brought all of life's ills on ourselves. Why should God be bothered with our problems?

But in fact, God is. God's heartbrokenness for human failure threads through all of Scripture. Therefore, following his example, God's people must be blame-LESS and care-FULL. Reflective, God-honoring souls must realize their own faults, silence their judgmental attitudes, and embrace the broken-hearted.

Reflections

1. *"Smart people sidestep pain."* Is this a true statement? If it is true, how do you differentiate between 'smart people' and 'caring people'?

2. *"One technique people often use to keep pain at a distance is questioning—especially the kind that focuses on facts."* Compare this statement with the opening statement of the book (*People need intimacy, not answers.*) and describe how the two intersect or relate.

3. *"Surely an uncaring question in the face of such heartbreak."* Why would someone ask, "Was he wearing a helmet?" when hearing of a fatal motorcycle accident?

4. *"Kindly people often wing arrows of blame into already wounded hearts through seemingly innocuous inquiries."* Make a list of comments you have made or remarks that you have heard that would be examples of this statement.

5. *"Human beings have a compulsion to complete the picture...We probe relentlessly for facts."* How difficult is it for you to postpone your questions until a later time and to listen, instead, to the feelings of the hurting person?

6. *"What value does this information have to the inquirer?"* What do you usually want to know when you hear that someone has died?

7. *"If we reserve compassion for the truly innocent, few are going to be worthy."* Not wearing a seat-belt; smoking; alcoholism; over-eating — how many other common human errors, accidents, or failures can you add to the list? Do they matter?

8. *"God's heartbrokenness for human failure threads through all of Scripture. If God cries over our hurts, we should also strive to show compassion to those around us."* Describe your agreement or disagreement with these two broad statements.

Chapter 5

Act Friendly Anyway

Some folks inherit shyness. For them socializing is a burden. Most people, though, slip into unsociable habits and patterns from busyness, forgetfulness, and self-centeredness.

Obligations accompany membership in the Christian community. High on the list is friendliness. But cheerful greetings and random acts of kindness depend on decisions, not just on the feelings of the moment. Good deeds cannot wait until the matching mood arises.

How to increase global warming

I have several major supermarkets to choose from when I contemplate my weekly foray into the grocery world. Sales and specials attract me toward one. Double coupons seduce me toward another. The free blood-pressure machine is a draw too. But usually I gravitate toward the store where there is an employee who regularly acts as if she is glad to see me. She stands out like a lighthouse on a rocky, barren coastline. She radiates hospitality.

She is truly unusual in the marketplaces I frequent. Other employees offer the mandatory eye contact and 'hello' required by the management. It is better than nothing, but not much. Mostly they appear as grim functionaries, just making a living.

One day I lingered to investigate the source and power shining from the 'lighthouse.' I complimented her, telling her how much I appreciated the warmth she exuded and what a difference it made. Then I pushed a little further, inquiring how it was that she gave so much, so warmly. I was hoping, of course, that she would say, "Well, I'm a Christian."

"Oh, I get it from my dad," she quipped breezily. "He's the same way."

I replied, "I thought maybe it came from being a Christian." "Well, I'm Catholic, but it comes from my dad," she said.

It does help to choose your parents carefully! A lot of the way we act derives from genetic and environmental sources. Taciturn parents often produce reserved children. Gregarious fathers regularly, but not always, bequeath society with outgoing sons.

But although it's true that some traits are carved in the genes or learned by example, as children of hope we must go beyond that. We can and must see our place in this world as a calling to be different. We are to display attitudes, values, and commitments that send the message that we march to a special drummer. Merely doing what comes naturally may not be good enough.

When traveling in Utah a few years ago, we stopped at a gas station. The car was serviced, the family refreshed, and we sped on our way again. A family member commented, "Those people running that station sure seemed different." Everyone agreed that they exuded conscientiousness, courtesy, kindness, and helpfulness. Then it dawned on me—we were in Mormon country. As unacceptable as their theology is, the Mormons at that station blessed us by their lives.

Another gas-station drama contrasts sharply with the one in Utah. The lady had a chrome-plated fish symbol neatly fixed to the back panel of her white Lincoln Continental. The name 'Jesus' was spelled out inside the lines defining the shape of the fish. It was right next to the license plate, which was framed by one of those clever sayings that starts on the top and finishes on the bottom. I could not see all of it, but on the lower part were the words, "You're Not Much."

The whole scene stands fixed in my memory because the driver, a large blond woman, was very upset with the gas-station attendant. He, a small Asian person, had accidentally spilled oil on the fender and motor of her beautiful car in the process of adding some to the crankcase. A hot verbal interchange ensued. Just before she slammed her door and sped away in a huff, the woman bellowed, "Vell, vy don't you people go back to your own country!"

I hoped the attendant did not notice the Jesus sign on the back of the car. It was a pathetic scene, but I couldn't keep from laughing at the irony of her words. She had a Christian label on her automobile, but her soul was sour.

Instead of nastiness, people need personal attention and unsolicited kindness. They crave spirit-lifting, heartache-healing, attitude-adjusting, and confidence-building. But there is a drought of such caring service. Showers of blessings sprinkle down all too rarely. Loneliness and hardness, harshness and indifference, fear and worry are more characteristic of humanity.

Every child of God must try a little harder to express the hopefulness we know. The Lord desires that we forget ourselves and think of others.

Indulging ourselves in bad moods should be forbidden when other people cross our paths.

The Manager of public relations for the Christian community expects his representatives to display the new life humming inside them. While "greeting each other with a holy kiss" may not always fit in our culture, we should act warm and friendly— even when we don't feel like it.

A friend of mine met a customer in his store one day who wore a colorful button on her lapel. It read, "Act Like You're Glad To See Me." The human race cries for more such attention.

Entering an unfamiliar church recently, I noticed a young couple standing near the sanctuary entrance. I reasoned they were the greeters of the day. Clearly timid, they nearly let us pass without a word. They did not act as if they were glad to see us.

As Christians, we must push out of our comfort zones. We must give what is needed and not stay where we are. Every human being on earth craves care in some form. Christian people, connected as they are to love's source, must let it flow freely through them, producing much-needed global warming.

Reflections

1. *"Some folks inherit shyness. Most people, though, slip into unsociable habits and patterns from busyness, forgetfulness, and self-centeredness."* Describe where you fit on this scale from shyness to busyness.

2. *"Good deeds cannot wait until the matching mood arises."* Tell of a time when you did a good deed, or offered a kindness, even though you weren't feeling in the mood to do so.

3. *"'Oh, I get it from my dad,' she quipped breezily. 'He's the same way.'"* Where does your cheerfulness come from? Do you think your friendliness is inherited, or learned? Is it a conscious effort you make, or does it come naturally?

4. *"She had a Christian label on her automobile, but her soul was sour."* What things in your life put a label on you? Are you conscious of the fact that you do indeed wear a label? How does that affect your words and your actions?

5. *"We should act warm and friendly— even when we don't feel like it."* What do you think of this statement?

6. *"Act Like You're Glad To See Me."* How is this little statement a guide for our interaction with other people?

7. *"As Christians, we must push out of our comfort zones."* Where are the boundaries of your comfort zone?

Chapter 6

You Need To Take A Closer Look

"He who answers before listening—that is his folly and his shame" (Prov. 18 : 13). This proverb rings true. It speaks of passing judgment without adequate data, of making decisions while lacking accurate information.

Strongly held opinions usually get undermined as both sides of a story play out. And they should. Truth mostly rests in the middle, seldom at the outer extremes.

With the questionable behaviors and the bothersome issues of life, tentativeness fits better than dogmatism, a moderate viewpoint better than unwavering certitude. Compassion and empathy accomplish the most enduring results when endeavoring to change the changeable.

Everything looks different close-up

It's easy to have all the answers from a distance, but "black" and "white" are harder to distinguish close-up.

Depression

Joe and Lena had definite ideas about why people become depressed. "Lack of faith" was their agreed-on diagnosis. To hear them talk, both prevention and cure should not be difficult—"Get right with God."

Then their married granddaughter slid into a long, stubborn, life-stifling depression. Slowly, reluctantly, but eventually, Joe and Lena changed their tune. They knew the young woman's spiritual commitments. Faithlessness was not the issue. Reduced to sad uncertainty and puzzlement, they modified their view on this illness.

Divorce

Ruth and Ben celebrated forty years of marriage. They had raised four children. Both the parents and their children claimed strong Christian views of marriage. Divorce happened to other people, unbelievers mostly. They saw no place for divorce, accepted no excuse for one, and had no tolerance for any. "If people love each other, fear the Lord, and keep their commitments, divorces need never occur."

In spite of lofty convictions, their oldest son left his wife. Reconciliation efforts failed, and a divorce followed. Ruth and Ben think differently now about divorced people. Compassion and understanding have crept into their hearts.

Homosexuality

John and Helen exemplify solid Christian people. In their sincere, God-honoring efforts, they often cited biblical evidence to support their dogmatic condemnation of homosexuals.

Then someone they loved revealed her gay sexual orientation. John and Helen cling to their convictions, but quietly now, and tentatively. Homosexuality no longer looms as a detested abstraction. It's someone they love.

* * *

The list has no end. Name a problem, and those who have only studied, read, or heard about it can prescribe the solution and boldly state God's attitude. Meanwhile, those personally challenged struggle, muddle, and suffer.

Surprisingly, some things look clear from a distance. Pictures focus differently close-up. Maybe both views are necessary. Truth and understanding often cannot be found when we stand either too far away or too close.

Standing too close, parents have even been known to shelter their criminal children and deny their wrongdoing. We can overlook a multitude of wrongs out of sheer sympathy for someone we love.

But the majority of human beings instinctively judge from a distance. Persons facing psychiatric problems, divorce, bankruptcy, suicide, addictions, unemployment, homosexuality, abortion, and similar challenges find little compassion from most well-functioning adults. Such conditions and circumstances look like weakness, irresponsibility, wrongness. Care and compassion, the strong ones believe, only make them multiply.

None of these conditions can be understood from the outside. Each feels sticky, complicated, terribly difficult, and painful up close. When we truly want to understand, we need to approach the afflicted ones, get close to those we judge and condemn, even though opening our minds and hearts in this way usually leads to contradiction of our dogmatic beliefs.

Consider the pastor who sits with any one of these strugglers in their private dilemmas and personal anguish, bleeding with the wounded, agonizing with the erroneous, walking with the offensive, listening to the divergent. Such close involvement leads to love, compassion, understanding—seldom to blanket condemnation.

Church members implore pastors to preach strongly against divorce, homosexuality, alcoholism. But to the pastor, these are not abstract dangers. He knows, loves, and struggles with warm Christian human beings caught in the webs of these circumstances. Each issue has become too complex and personal to simply preach against.

Judging others is clearly intolerable. When we do it from a detached and distant viewpoint, we are arrogant and ignorant. But, sad to say, when we attempt to sort things out from the inside, hearing the whole story, facing the individual eye-to-eye with heart engaged, right from wrong is difficult to discern. Truly credible and acceptable positions emerge only from walking hand-in-hand or sitting face-to-face with searching souls.

The way of God is not the way of conventional force and distant observation. Close-up is the way of the cross. Christ enters our suffering, suffers with us, and changes our hearts from the inside out. He dies for us and with us. That is the only way!

But getting close usually hurts. It means we must honestly recognize sin in ourselves. It requires taking on some of the suffering of another person. Our confidence will be shaken, our certitude bowled over.

Still then, and only then, is there possibility for healing, helping, restoring.

Reflections

1. *"Compassion and empathy accomplish the most enduring results..."* How would you define or describe the word 'empathy'?

2. *"Several life challenges were discussed: Depression, Divorce, Homosexuality."* Which are the most difficult for you to understand and accept? Of these challenges (or others that should be added to the list), which ones are you closest to? Please share your connection.

3. *"Truth and understanding often cannot be found when we stand either too far away or too close."* What do you think it means to stand too close, or to stand too far away?

4. *"But the majority of human beings instinctively judge from a distance ... and find little compassion from most well-functioning adults."* Do you agree with this statement? Why do you think this is true (or not true)?

5. *"Truly credible and acceptable positions emerge only from walking hand-in-hand or sitting face-to-face with searching souls."* Describe a situation when you experienced walking hand-in-hand with a hurting person.

6. *"Close-up is the way of the cross."* What does this statement mean to you? Whom have you recently judged from a distance?

7. *"But getting close usually hurts."* How is this statement a reflection of the story of the Dun Cow in Chapter 1? Describe how this relates to Question #2 above.

Chapter 7

Speedy Escapes Deprive Us Of Vital Lessons

A perfectly natural reflex moves us quickly away from painful and dangerous circumstances. It works to save lives and maintain emotional equilibrium. Looking the other way, blocking out sad thoughts, avoiding horrible scenes—all often make sense in our efforts to keep a positive outlook or just to guarantee a restful night of sleep.

But there is a time to mourn and feel deeply too. Now and then avoidance must be set aside to let the full impact of life's realities hit home. Then we grow and become more human, more credible, deeper and richer.

The joy and sorrow of changing a light bulb

Do you know how many country-music singers it takes to change a light bulb? Five. One to change the bulb. Four to sing about how much they miss the old one.

After almost thirty years with at least one youngster present, our house was suddenly childless. I could have used a country music group to sing some blues about the emptiness we felt after our youngest child left the nest. Nurturing our children, the most important task God gave us, was now finished. For nearly three decades, everything else ranked secondary. Adjusting to this completion presented a serious challenge.

Not that our last departing teenager was lively company those last few years. Some weeks he hardly talked more than to give a reluctant greeting and farewell. His life was elsewhere, with his friends, as it should have been. Home supplied basic physical necessities. At age eighteen his balance seemed appropriate.

In order for you to understand how things were with our little family group, I present this anecdote: One night at the dinner table I described a pastoral encounter I had had earlier in the day. It was a real-life family drama. At stake was the decision of whether or not to take the father of the family off a life-support system, which was sustaining him in his comatose condition. This gigantic dilemma slammed down hard on his three adult children.

As I finished telling this story, suddenly and surprisingly, our teenager awakened. "What did you recommend?" he asked. When I told him I favored disconnecting the machines, he protested: "I don't think that's right. Inside that person is a real live human being with thoughts, feelings, and interests."

At this point I couldn't resist a humorous comment. With tongue in cheek, I replied, "You know, Steve, I think you are right.

I know I assume it is true of you." For that I earned one of the rare, prized rewards of parenthood. In spite of his best efforts, Steve cracked an amused grin. Today I realize how much I enjoyed those occasional breakthroughs and miss the opportunity to try for them.

A few days after our son moved out, I told some colleagues that our youngest had left for college and that I struggled uncomfortably with the adjustment. "Enjoy it!" cried one. "Oh, this is the best time of your life," said another. "You'll get used to this real fast," laughed a third. "Forget it," advised my remaining counselor.

It struck me then, and I said so, that I didn't appreciate their advice: "I know I'll get used to it. I also know this ushers in a great new chapter for us. And I do plan to enjoy it. In fact, I'm enjoying it already and anticipating a lot of wonderful new freedoms. But right now I also want to experience my grief. I want to feel bad and sad. The end of something really big and important just happened, and I don't care to glide past the sobering reality of it as if it doesn't exist." My colleagues didn't know what to say to this strange spiel, so I went on. "I don't want to rush on and miss the lessons waiting here for me."

"Like what?" laughed a skeptic.

"Well," I said, "like getting a tiny glimpse of what it must be like when someone's child departs in death and will never come back. I feel the tears well up now, and my kid is merely going off to college. So that's something. I'm growing some new compassion."

Our brown-bag luncheon had gotten way too serious. By unspoken consensus our conversation drifted to something lighter, but my outlook and intentions stayed the same.

I do not believe we act wisely when we slip too smoothly over the significant transitional events of life. Whether it is the first child going to kindergarten or off to military service, to college or to her own apartment, these are moments to ponder. They will soon enough be swept up and away in our

43

busyness. So it is important to linger with them, to feel the feelings—sadness, pride, satisfaction, joy, relief, loneliness, and exhilaration.

There are other things that changed for me too. I miss the help: I dislike washing cars, and I had to hire a lawn service. I miss the company too: With whom do I talk and watch sports? Who will listen to my dumb jokes? I also miss the excitement of my child's life—his growth, development, friendships, and activities. The nest sits empty. Yes, I'm enjoying it very much. But I also feel sad.

"Teach us to number our days," prays the psalmist (Ps. 90:12). Reflecting and ruminating on major life changes helps us to do so. Pondering about endings and beginnings brings home the richness of life's onward surges. Feeling the poignancy of passing time, of pages turned and new chapters opened, seasons life with thanksgiving. Remembering brings to life the past and equips for the future.

If we truly "number our days," we won't let events pass by thoughtlessly; we will feel their impact and process them thoughtfully in order to gain the wisdom God wants us to gain. Transitions never cease. Changes never end. But people of faith trust that "the best is yet to be"—even though we let go of the old things reluctantly.

Reflections

1. *"I struggled uncomfortably with the adjustment. 'Enjoy it!' cried one. 'You'll get used to this real fast,' laughed a third."* Why did these well-intentioned remarks fall flat?

2. *"But right now I also want to experience my grief."* Why would a person WANT to embrace grief?

3. *"The end of something really big and important just happened..."* Share any meaningful 'endings' in your life. Recall important personal endings that were ignored, or made light of.

4. *"We slip too smoothly over the significant transitional events of life."* What does this mean? What examples of this can you list?

5. *"'Teach us to number our days,' prays the psalmist (Ps. 90:12)."* Explain what you think the psalmist meant by 'numbering our days.'

6. *"Pondering about endings and beginnings brings home the richness of life's onward surges. Feeling the poignancy of passing time, of pages turned and new chapters opened, seasons life with thanksgiving."* Share your attitude and feelings about attending funerals and memorial services. What are your ideas and plans for your own funeral?

7. *"Transitions never cease. Changes never end."* How well do you accept the changes that life brings? How do you fight off the changes that come? What kind of changes do you anticipate and embrace?

Chapter 8

Every Person Is A Potential Healer

Life and death crises cry out for more than excellent medical care. As spiritual-physical organisms, humans respond positively to the mysterious but powerful influence of smiles, encouragement, touch, and even the sight of caring friends.

When people are sick or injured, the work of physicians and nurses often helps the patients to regain renewed health. But love, in its many expressions, provides the fuel for true recovery. Personal care glues the wounded together again.

How ordinary people helped save a life

D r. Gordon Hondorp and his wife, Mary Lou, were in Anaheim, California, for a medical conference in March 1993. Shortly after a dinner they were driving to another destination when a speeding car ignored a red light and broad-sided them. The crash struck the driver's side, smashing Gordon viciously. Mary Lou was seriously injured; Gordon, critically.

An ambulance rushed them to the University of California Irvine Medical Center, where outstanding care stood ready. Mary Lou's broken bones healed on schedule. She soon left hospital care to stand by in support of her husband.

At first Gordon was alert and responsive, and even though he was in very critical condition, he observed and communicated while the attending physicians and staff worked.

I visited Gordon and Mary Lou during those early days of crisis. And when I saw how Gordon made it through the early crisis and continued responding, I thought he'd be OK. I left on a week of vacation feeling reassured about the Hondorps.

When I returned, I was shocked to learn of Gordon's badly deteriorating physical condition. At least a dozen tubes entered and exited his body. He was conscious, but, due to the ventilator and tubes, was unable to speak. His body appeared inflated with air—swollen and distorted. Infections and fungi swarmed inside of him. His overloaded respiratory system and heart, along with practically every other bodily system, struggled. Survival looked doubtful. For days, then weeks, his condition worsened.

All the while a vast network of family, friends, and strangers prayed. People from all over North America offered prayers for the seemingly dying man.

The Hondorps' church sent delegates to stand by and pray. The pastor himself made two trips, including one on Good Friday, when the outlook appeared most bleak.

The Hondorps' family of adult children camped in the hospital. But no evidence of victory glimmered.

Finally on the Monday after Easter, more than six weeks after the accident, a spark of hope appeared. Gordon started improving.

After another few weeks crawled by, Gordon and his wife limped home to Palo Alto, California. The intensive care unit had cradled him for a total of sixty days, most of them bleak.

What saved Gordon Hondorp's life?

A university hospital is a good place to be in dire circumstances. Without a doubt the outstanding medical resources available at UCI played a major role in saving Gordon's life. But there were about five other pieces in the recovery package:

- The wonderful, mysterious power of prayer. This can be understood simply as God answering the cries of many. Or, as I prefer, God transmitting healing sustenance through the prayer-focused hearts, minds, and wills of caring people, who are purposefully concentrating their intercessions on a sorely wounded child of God.

- The loving, tender presence of family and friends throughout the ordeal. Imagine the spirit-lifting difference the touches and smiles of Gordon's children made. Love cannot be quantified like the fluids and medicines dripping in and out of Gordon's body, but there exists no more powerful healing elixir than a loving presence in the time of trouble.

- Loneliness, fear, despair, and anger are some of the gravest enemies of health and healing. The bedside faithfulness of caring people dissipates and mollifies these spirit-sucking infections better than anything. Without the visible and audible support of his family, Gordon's weakened body would have had even more to overcome and less spirit with which to fight. Visible love generates hope. Hope maintains life.

- The chemistry-enhancing qualities of encouraging words. Encouraging words do more than enter the ear and get recorded on the brain's register of memories. Words change the body's chemistry. Honest, reassuring words are biochemical realities that trigger positive healing secretions. Good words restore health and fight infections.

- The will to live. After he left the hospital, Gordon said, "Through it all, I never expected to die." He had a high measure of hopefulness, nourished by prayer, the presence of loved ones, and their spirit-lifting words.

  On the other hand, Gordon admitted that, in the middle of the relentless suffering, he thought more than once, "Maybe I should just give up." His weary body cried strongly to give up, to stop striving to stay alive. But at some deeper level his feverish soul negated that idea and fought on to victory.

- The wondrous recuperative potential in the human body. Certainly there lies ahead for all of us the time in which the body will fail. However, in the span between birth and death, the astoundingly resilient physical/spiritual system stages many comebacks from the insults and injuries inflicted on it.

Gordon Hondorp recuperates at home now, saved by wise and crafty medical staff, the amazing human body, and the power of God in response to his caring people. And we all give thanks.

Reflections

1. *"God transmitting healing sustenance"* Tell about any remarkable healing experiences you have either been close to or heard about.

2. *"The wonderful, mysterious power of prayer."* Share an instance of how prayer was answered dramatically for you. What do you think about the idea of God healing through our prayer?

3. *"The loving, tender presence of family and friends"* 90% of helping is just showing up! Describe a particular time when you witnessed the healthful impact made by the presence of family and friends.

4. *"The bedside faithfulness of caring people . . ."* In a hospital visit, describe how you feel: stiff, relaxed, apprehensive? When talking to the families of the sick, what is your approach? Are you friendly, or hurried? Are you interested and caring?

5. *"The bedside faithfulness of caring people . . ."* If the doctors told you that you were dying, what are some things you would want your family and friends to do for you?

Chapter 9

The Player And The Umpire See The Game Differently

Peak performers concentrate on the game, not the rules. They give their all, keeping the rules instinctively, erring unintentionally. Umpires seldom enjoy the game, focused as they are on infractions, violations, and boundary lines.

Umpires fill a need in athletic competition, but umpire-like friends and family members alienate and irritate. The game of life sails most smoothly when players self-officiate rather than when others blow whistles at them.

Society needs some whistle-blowers. So do children up to a point. But the self-appointed ones assessing everything miss the game!

Are you an umpire or a player?

An old speech class illustration tells of a clergyman who created an attention-getting opener for his sermon: "It's a _ _ _ _ hot day," he cried out as his opener. He paused for a moment, then continued: " . . . I heard a man say as I left my house a few minutes ago."

Predictably that pastor riveted everybody's attention. From that point on, I guess, some listened intently and profited from the message. Others, shocked to attention in that way, heard no more. That one profanity branded into their brains remained until they unloaded on the church council with their fervent lament about such sinful talk.

Clever, but not a wise move on the pastor's part. He may have delivered a potentially life-changing sermon that the most needful were incapable of receiving, preoccupied as they were with the one bad word.

Some people trundle through life like umpires. They see everything through judgmental spectacles—assessing; evaluating; weighing people, events, actions, words. All the time they're making calls: "Right! Wrong! Good! Bad! Smart! Stupid! Liberal! Conservative!"

- Jennifer's mother scolds, "You shouldn't have been over there in the first place," when her daughter runs home crying after a fall in the neighbor's driveway.

- Garrick listens to Sunday sermons faithfully and inevitably gives his stamp of approval or disapproval. "He hit the target today." Or, "He certainly put little time into that one."

- When Bentley hears his hospitalized neighbor has cirrhosis of the liver, his initial feeling of concern dissipates. "He has to be an alcoholic. I have no sympathy for him."

- Pastor Verdue sees nothing but a sinful attitude when parishioner Holum shares, "I'm sorry my mother died. It deprives me of the chance to let her know how much I despised her."

Umpires run alongside the players, watchful, but not part of the game. They are out of the action. They stand by themselves. They know the rules but miss the real game.

- Jennifer's mother sidesteps her daughter's distress. She reacts dispassionately. Trespassing and rule-breaking concern her.

- Garrick's soul, preoccupied with evaluation, remains untouched by messages from the pulpit. Style, delivery, accuracy, and orthodoxy dominate his consciousness.

- Bentley judges the alcoholic as bad, stupid, and wrong.

- Such folks deserve no mercy. They are "out," relegated to the trash pile.

- Pastor Verdue, preoccupied with right and wrong, lacks the capability to hear and feel the deeper issues of Mrs. Holum's agony.

Knowing right from wrong remains a fundamental human virtue. Without the capacity for such discernment, a person is in grave danger. But to be a truly compassionate friend, each of us, blessed with the knowledge of good and evil, must regularly set judgment aside.

To truly see persons—to weep with those who weep, to be touched and broken for loved ones—we must exercise the capacity to overlook, at least for a while, questions of right and wrong, good and bad, excellent or faulty. To love my neighbor, my child, my friends, the gas station attendant, the store clerk, and anyone else who comes into my daily life, I need to see creatures of God trying to live their best.

Are we umpires or players? Do we stand apart, or are we in the game? Some Christians believe they are called to officiate at the game of life rather than to participate fully in it. They major in calling errors, fouls, penalties, balks—mostly on others, but often on themselves as well.

Players, usually mindful of their own inadequacies and shortcomings, criticize each other reluctantly. They pat each other on the backside and speak reassuring words about mistakes and goofs.

I've never forgotten the couplet penned by Edwin Markham on this subject:

> Heretic, rebel, a thing to flout—
> We drew a circle to keep him out.
> But love and I had the wit to win;
> We drew a circle to bring him in.

Umpires call people out. Players bring people in.

Reflections

1. *"Performers concentrate on the game...umpires focus on infractions, violations, and boundary lines."* Describe whether you are a performer or an umpire in life and to what degree.

2. *"Performers concentrate on the game...umpires focus on infractions, violations, and boundary lines."* Reflect on your parent's role in your life in regard to the 'umpire-player' idea.

3. *"Some people trundle through life like umpires. They see everything through judgmental spectacles."* What kind of strange or inappropriate words, talk, or behavior, is likely to bother and/or distract you?

4. *"Knowing right from wrong remains a fundamental human virtue."* How do you separate this as a virtue from its tendency to often get in the way of a compassion attitude?

5. *"...to weep with those who weep."* How do you do this? Share an instance where you feel you truly wept with another person.

6. *"I need to see creatures of God trying to live their best."* How well do you feel that you are doing at seeing everyday people (the grocery clerk, the mechanic, the bank teller) as people who face the same difficulties as you?

Chapter 10

Wake-Up Calls Irritate, But Enlighten, Too

When earthquakes, floods, tornadoes, and other disasters hit population centers, they take a harsh toll on people and property. Almost always, however, the victims bounce or struggle back and emerge stronger, wiser, deeper, better.

The spiritual benefits of close calls add up steadily for those who are knocked to their knees. They meet God, reassess their own limitations, and grow.

A mild earthquake is good for the soul

It hit with a house-rocking 'wham!' We were jolted into full consciousness from a dead sleep. "Earthquake!" we said needlessly to each other as the room swayed. I jumped out of bed and pulled on my jeans.

Down the hall Steve's light glowed, but he was calmly lying in bed. "How come you're dressed?" he said. "What are you doing?"

"I don't know," I replied. "It just seems that I should be doing something." But even as I said it, I realized Steve's attitude made sense. Usually when an earthquake comes, there's nothing to do but go back to sleep.

I find earthquakes more unsettling than tornadoes, floods, and fires. Even though the damage from those acts of nature is always horrifying, they allow us to retain some sense of control. Early warnings and alarms often announce their approach. We are able to run, hide, and evade, or at least we have the illusion that we can.

Earthquakes slam in unannounced. They just happen— suddenly! There is no place to hide, no way to elude, nowhere to go. Everything shakes and rolls. Nothing stands secure and solid. Terrified, we wonder, is there another tremor still coming? Will it be a big one? THE BIG ONE? Earthquakes shake us to the core because they short-circuit our inner security systems. The notion of being in charge of one's personal safety gets knocked off its foundation. Helplessness defines the moment.

Life is dangerous, but God has ingeniously clothed us in protective garb called "repression and denial." Those mortal garments enable us to enjoy life rather fully even as they cover up how naked and exposed we really are. Sometimes we take God's gifts of repression and denial beyond their intended purpose, and we ride without seat belts, take the batteries out of smoke detectors, inhale cigarette smoke, or ignore high cholesterol levels and elevated blood pressures.

With its jolting and shaking, an earthquake, like a burglary or a rape, violently strips away our protective armor—the notion that we are safe and in control. Earthquakes disillusion us. They rob us of our fantasies of invulnerability.

Someone has observed that the psychotic person is not out of touch with reality—just the opposite. The plight of the mentally ill, according to this view, is that their protective denial system has failed. They are haunted by how dangerous life is, how frail and mortal they are. The so-called healthy folks keep harsh realities buried, ignored, and repressed, and thus are able to live as if they are immortal. Denying danger, they carry on as if nothing could happen to them.

At times in California "tremblers," as little shakers are called, and the constant threat and talk of the inevitable BIG ONE tend to erode people's usual sense of security. Some older folks, whose personal vulnerability has been aggravated by the loss of spouse, health, or physical agility, are rumored to be sleeping fully dressed and even on couches close to the doors of their houses.

Natural disasters are not good. We cannot simplistically say they are from God. The damage, death, and destruction they bring are too sad and terrible for anything but lament and anguish. It is distressing to see little children, older folks, or anyone lose zest for life because they are fearfully expecting disaster. For those paralyzed with apprehension we pray that God's implanted denial system may once again activate so that they can live again as if they are safe.

Nevertheless an eye-opening jolt of 5.5 on the Richter scale facilitates needed awakening for people whose denial systems work too well. Cruising along, completely immune and detached, and thinking that bad things happen only to other people is an illness itself. Earthquakes, for most of us, work as an effective temporary cure for a sense of security so smug that even our reach toward God becomes perfunctory.

When there is no place to hide and nothing to be done, when everything could shake apart or crash down on top of us in a few seconds, we quickly recognize our only true security. Few things focus the mind as well as a middle-sized earthquake. It instantaneously clarifies what really lasts, what cannot be broken or taken away.

Reflections

1. *"Earthquakes disillusion us."* What is it about an earthquake that makes us feel out of control? Why do we fear being out of control?

2. *"A mild earthquake is good for the soul?"* How do you react to this title for the chapter?

3. *"They rob us of our fantasies of invulnerability."* Have you ever had an 'earthquake' in your life that caused you to see your true security differently? When? How?

4. *"With its jolting and shaking, an earthquake, like a burglary or a rape, violently strips away our protective armor—the notion that we are safe and in control."* Tell about any deep, or mild, fears or anxieties you have, and live with.

5. *"Safe in the arms of Jesus"* What do these words mean to you?

Chapter 11

Generous Giving Has Limitations

Those who live exclusively on the one-way street of giving pay a high price. Receiving balances giving. The energy and enthusiasm people need for constant giving dwindles unless it is replenished by a willing reception of kindness.

All giving and no receiving eventually embitters the generous soul. A lifetime of spirited giving depends on feeling one's own wants now and then and humbly accepting another's gifts and care. "Givers must receivers be."

Giving is great, but receiving is essential, too

Milly eats the burned toast. The family gets the good slices. She always takes the scrawniest pork chop and sits in the back seat, or wherever no one else wants to sit. When a child is ill, she alone gets up at night to look after the little one. She and her husband occasionally eat out and take in a movie. Milly defers to her husband's preferences, insisting convincingly that it really doesn't matter to her where they go. On birthdays and at Christmas Milly has no needs, makes no lists, claims she has everything. Milly is also extraordinarily attentive to her neighbors and extended family. Weekly she teaches Sunday school and volunteers at the community hospital.

This kind of exemplary living has a downside. All giving gradually creates numbness toward one's own needs. Constant caretaking of others, along with denial of personal discomforts and desires, creates a kind of non-person. It may be better to give than to receive, but all giving and no receiving shrivels the soul.

Someone has described a primary task of life as "growing soul." It isn't easy to define exactly what this means, but the phrase is a good one. It implies becoming more of a person—deeper and wiser—and becoming more human, more real. These are all indefinable goals, but still recognizably good.

Small-souled people come in a variety of sizes, shapes, and tastes, but one common feature they display is not needing anybody or anything. Self-sufficiency describes them. They surround themselves with high-walled blockades. Often hostile, they live as if prepared for a lifetime under siege. To survive, they have cut off all emotional supply lines. They nourish themselves from their own dehydrated food as best they can.

The more common soul-starved people are those who live active participatory lives. Their life scripts instruct them to love everybody, to help, to heal, to fix. They may be physicians, pastors, counselors, mothers, plumbers, mechanics, or anything else. Caretaking defines them. Caretakers, whether professional or amateur, answer the questions of others, solve their problems, sacrifice. They are givers. Caretakers bless those around them. They see to it that conditions are comfortable and enjoyable for each person who enters their sphere of influence. Full-time caretaking, however, slowly sucks the life from the giver. This one-sided lifestyle keeps someone from staying in touch with her own needs. Milly, the burned-toast eater, eventually moves around robotically—flat, uninteresting, mechanical.

Soul-care depends on knowing one's own neediness. The life that grows out of touch with one's own heartaches, loneliness, hungers, thirsts, desires, likes, and dislikes, loses its humanness and part of its godliness as well.

Givers must learn to be receivers. Only those with needs open themselves to receiving. For a person to grow soul, receiving is essential. To receive, one must want something, one must be more than a unilateral lover. Healthy souls ask for help and let others help them. They like things, have preferences, and allow themselves to be cared for.

Our Lord models a life of balanced giving and receiving. Often we speak of the ideal love as agape, which is selfless, all-giving love; yet in Jesus' brief career on earth he did not exclusively give love to others. His giving was punctuated by appropriate self-concern. He showed neediness. He got tired and escaped from the masses. He hungered and thirsted. He felt let down. He cried out when he felt abandoned. He asked for help. He enjoyed being alone with his most intimate friends. He sorrowed, shed tears of grief, expressed exasperation. He relished special affection. The God of Scripture is not a love machine but a person wracked with our pain, thrilled with our joys, affected deeply by our care or carelessness, needfully receiving as well as giving.

Eventually Milly disappeared as a person to her family and friends. Her children took advantage of her. She had trained them not to think of her needs or to consider her in their planning. She became invisible. Little of the milk of human kindness flowed her way because she never longed for anything, never lacked or preferred. In the business of caretaking and giving, she glossed over her own needs until they disappeared and she with them.

Realness must emerge, or soul death happens. Realness means asking for help. It means having dislikes and liking nice things. It means having opinions and wanting to go places and do things.

It means staking a claim for oneself as a child of God, a child to be taken seriously.

Reflections

1. *"Givers must receivers be."* Do you find it harder to receive gestures and kindnesses from others than to give them out? Why do you think people have difficulty with this issue? Describe your own needs and wants.

2. *"Someone has described a primary task of life as 'growing soul.'"* Restate in your own words what you think this means? How does one go about growing the soul?

3. *"Self-sufficient people surround themselves with high-walled blockades. To survive, they have cut off all emotional supply lines."* When is self-sufficiency considered to be a negative attribute? Can you describe a viewpoint where it could be a positive characteristic?

4. *"Milly has no needs, makes no lists, claims she has everything... Eventually Milly disappeared as a person to her family and friends."* Do you know someone like Milly? What stories can you relate about her?

5. *"Realness means asking for help."* How comfortable are you at asking for help? Why is it hard for so many people to do?

6. *"The God of Scripture is not a love machine but a person wracked with our pain, thrilled with our joys, affected deeply by our care or carelessness."* How comfortable are you with the claims that God hurts <u>with</u> you, and rejoices when <u>you do</u>?

Chapter 12

Resurrection Power Works Wonders Every Day

Some people bounce back from the most unbelievable tragedies. Some others, though, get permanently sidelined from seemingly minor hardships. These few get stuck, mystifying loved ones who futilely urge them to move on.

Big deaths and small deaths happen all the time. They range from the untimely loss of loved ones, to financial setbacks, to the demise of long-held hopes and dreams. All are death-like in their impact.

To start up again challenges every survivor. Any kind of loss dispirits a person; it weakens the will, saps physical strength, and lowers immunity to all kinds of dangers, both bodily and spiritual.

In the strength and spirit of Christ, who defeated big death, God's people are called to get up and start over after every death. Deaths big and small must not win. As hard as comebacks may be, resurrection people make them.

After a hurricane, search for flowers

H urricane Hugo ripped through the Caribbean National Forest of
Puerto Rico in September 1989, bulldozing most of the stunning
canopy of trees and other flora and fauna.

That spectacular woods had thrived as a densely packed umbrella of beauty
for hundreds of years, but fierce winds of up to 212 miles per hour totally
wiped out this glorious gem of creation.

That spectacular woods had thrived as a densely packed umbrella of beauty
for hundreds of years, but fierce winds of up to 212 miles per hour totally
wiped out this glorious gem of creation.

Months later something surprising began to happen. As sunlight illuminated
what used to be the forest floor, seeds germinated and plants grew that had
not been seen in ages, some never before. According to the Los Angeles
Times, the director of the U.S. Forest Service's Institute of Tropical Forestry
said, "Thanks to the hurricane, we are seeing a far richer diversity of (plant)
species."

This paradoxical and heartwarming story from the world of nature parallels
human experience. No one would ever recommend cutting down or
burning the valued rainforests to raise the flowers Hurricane Hugo helped
germinate. Given a choice, most would prefer to restore the Caribbean
National Forest to its pre-hurricane beauty, even if they knew it eliminated
the possibility of seeing exotic fresh gifts spring up.

The same applies to the storms that sweep into the lives of God's children.
Nobody wants them. What they take away can never be replaced.

Rise up against the devastation of multiple sclerosis, leukemia, AIDS, birth
defects, and every other tragic intrusion! Fight every way possible to avert

divorce, bankruptcy, unemployment, and natural disaster. The possibility that something worthwhile might germinate after any of these heartaches triggers no appetite for a taste.

Sensible people never gladly open their arms to bad times, no matter what the potential fringe benefits might be. Nevertheless, in the personal experience of many, the catastrophes of life, once some time has passed, almost always have opened new vistas of growth previously unimagined.

A few weeks ago over breakfast, I met a healthy-looking, vivacious, middle-aged man. His positive outlook and hopeful attitude attracted me. As we talked, he told me how his highly successful life had been radically intruded on by the insidiously progressive illness of multiple sclerosis. But then he quickly added his parallel to the rainforest story. His present outlook on life, he said enthusiastically, was vastly richer and far more deeply satisfying than it was prior to his having MS. On the one hand, he said, he would give a fortune to have his full health back. On the other hand, the growth in his life made possible by the devastation of all he had relied on in the past is priceless to him. The disease brought wealth to his life beyond anything he had ever known.

Eventually past treasures must fade from view, allowing new visions to emerge. Single-minded grieving for the flattened forest simply blinds park lovers to thrilling new possibilities popping up around them. If all they see is fallen trees, they will never rejoice and embrace the new blossoms.

Likewise with my forward-looking friend. If his lost health was all he could see, then nothing but mourning could find a place in his heart. But by opening up to God's speaking to him in his affliction, he now celebrates exciting seeds germinating and bearing fruit all around him. When we look too narrowly or too long at what has been taken away, we will never see the fresh challenges God expects us to seize. When our focus sticks on the past, exciting new growth with the potential to enrich us and fledgling blessings waiting to hatch will slip by unused and wasted.

Here's how some Southern folks eventually learned how adversity could be a blessing. In the center of the town square in Enterprise, Alabama, stands a lofty monument. At the top rests the honored one—an insect, the boll weevil. Legions of this insidious pest had for many years wiped out the cotton crop in the South. Spring after spring farmers planted their seeds with

73

high hopes. Again and again the boll weevil ruined everything. Eventually the South caved in. People planted other crops and tried different approaches to making a living. Gradually a much improved economy emerged with the resiliency to sustain itself even when the cotton crop, or any other single venture, did not work out.

The people of Alabama woke up one day to the realization that the boll weevil had rendered them a valuable favor. The hated pest had forced them to diversify. When they relied on cotton alone, they were weak and vulnerable. Now they looked forward, strong and ready for adversity. And they owed it all to the dreaded insect and a willingness to change.

The most important insights about life trickle out of suffering. Depth of spirit and strength of character belong exclusively to the veterans of deep wounds. Grieving people gain exposure to the life-giving sun through the agonizing loss of what sheltered them. These folks are privy to knowledge that the safely harbored ones cannot acquire.

True, positive results do not always follow bad times. It is not easy to find a windfall in every ill breeze, especially when it thunders in as a hurricane or tornado. But for those who are challenged to see them and determined to grasp whatever they can of good in awful circumstances, flowers will emerge.

Unfortunately, most of the suffering people of this world do little more than suffer. Nothing beneficial or beautiful emerges from the ashes of their firestorms. They see nothing but clinkers and dust, and they have a bitter taste that won't go away. Consequently, most of the suffering in the world sits wasted. Searching and scavenging, not sitting, turn losses into gains. To uncover valuables in the rubble after the flames are extinguished calls for hard and dirty work.

Romans 5 : 3–4 gives us a tidy formula for our adversity recovery kit: "We also rejoice in our sufferings, because we know that suffering produces perseverance; perseverance, character; and character, hope."

When we struggle to our feet after being bowled over, we discover the possibility of starting over. Resurrections in everyday life generate confidence in bigger resurrections. Those who come back to life after seemingly mortal blows grow resurrection in their hearts and souls. They gain a hold on life the rest of us can't have until our hurricanes hit. They know hope personally.

Resurrections seldom proceed quickly and easily. Quick ones feel counterfeit and incredible. Most of the roads to joy stretch long, difficult, and slow. And the paths always pass through the village of suffering. Without a cross there is no resurrection. But with the Lord's help, life after death is guaranteed. In this life and the next.

Reflections

1. *"Any kind of loss dispirits a person; it weakens the will, saps physical strength..."* If it is difficult for you to describe your own losses, relate what you know about someone else who has faced a serious loss, and how they dealt with it.

2. *"The possibility that something worthwhile might germinate after any of these heartaches triggers no appetite for a taste."* Did the story about Hurricane Hugo affect your viewpoint of disasters? With the knowledge of outcomes such as this, why do you think we so quickly assume that any kind of heartache is purely bad? That nothing good can come of it?

3. *"The catastrophes of life, once some time has passed, almost always have opened new vistas of growth previously unimagined."* What situation can you recall where you have seen or experienced something good come out of what seemed so terrible at the time?

4. *"The disease brought wealth to his life beyond anything he had ever known."* Share how you grew or gained personally, in any way, from hurtful and unwanted distresses or losses in your life.

5. *"Most of the suffering in the world sits wasted... most of the suffering people of this world do little more than suffer."* What can we do for these people? How can they be helped to see the possibility of change for the good?

Chapter 13

There Is a Time To Give — And Ask No Questions

Little in life arrives with no strings attached. Human nature being what it is, gifts are not easily received or comfortably accepted by most. Repayment seems necessary whenever a kindness falls our way.

God's love stands above all gifts. Because it is offered freely, humankind need only accept and celebrate. But earthly distributors of God's love often complicate the offer—asking and even demanding certain behaviors or attitudes for another person to qualify. They turn a gift into a deal: "You give that, and God returns with this."

If we catch God's love directly, the life-changing effect is astonishing because love changes people. Instead of our changing to be loved, love changes us.

Opportunities often call for doing it God's way—just giving love away, no questions asked. Scary business. Hard to carry out. But it does happen.

A banquet
in West Hollywood

On Thursday, July 2, there was a phone message from Silver Lake, West Hollywood. A young man was dying of liver cancer. He requested a visit by a pastor, but the caller acknowledged that the sick man had not been in church for decades and had lived a wild life. Would we come anyway? Two of our seminary interns willingly agreed to go together. The call included a request for communion. We talked about the appropriateness of this and decided the dire circumstances called for going ahead with it. So off they went, Bibles and the portable communion kit in hand.

The interns found the home, a neatly kept condominium with modern decor and several autographed show-business photos on one of the walls. The sick man lay on a mattress on the floor in cheerful surroundings, accompanied by his mother and the friend who had called. Suddenly the seminarians knew they were visiting their first AIDS victim. And they realized, a fact confirmed later, that the caller didn't think the church would respond if he had said the man was dying of AIDS.

Kneeling on each side of the dying man, the interns introduced themselves. "How are you doing?" one asked.

The man's answer was the only word they would hear from him on this visit: "Terrible!" Later we all wondered about that one word. Was it only a reference to the physical condition? Or was it a spiritually significant cry? Most likely, we agreed, it was both. Here was a person in the throes of absolute affliction, physically and spiritually empty of any self-sustaining strength.

Then the festivities began. The seminarians showered the dying man with God's love in every way they could think of. One softly sang 'Amazing Grace,' and the others joined in. They read Psalm 23, assuring him of the companionship of the Good Shepherd, who was walking with him through the valley of the shadow of death. They fed him other soul-nourishing psalms and anointed his soul with the comforting promises of God's faithfulness and love.

They turned to the heartwarming eighth chapter of Romans: "If God is for us, who can be against us? . . . Christ Jesus, who died—more than that, who was raised to life—is at the right hand of God and is also interceding for us. Who shall separate us from the love of Christ?" (8 : 31–35). They held his hands and prayed that he would experience deep peace and feel, know, and experience the presence of Jesus at his side in this time of suffering.

Then the banquet! The feast was made ready. They brought it to him in the form of a tiny cracker dipped in grape juice and gently laid on his reaching tongue. The party ended with prayer and the Lord's Prayer quietly recited by the whole group. The guest of honor managed a slight smile and then rested.

Three days later the young seminarians officiated at the man's funeral. It was in the same spirit as the earlier Lord's Supper celebration. They shared the words and verses rich with God's love, grace, and presence to the wayward, weary, and forlorn. Except for the overriding sorrow and tragedy being keenly expressed by his friends and family, one could again pick up the banquet theme, the joy and excitement of the loving Father welcoming home a beloved child.

The next day second thoughts arrived. As we sat down to talk about the deep pool of ministry into which these young men had been unexpectedly submerged, doubts surfaced. The seminarians began to wonder if they should have first obtained more information about the dying man and inquired about his spiritual condition. Maybe they should at least have tried to get a clue of his assent to all they'd given him. Perhaps they should have asked for a squeeze of the hand or a blink of the eyes to indicate that he indeed loved the Lord and was sorry for his sins. The joy of the event was becoming clouded by querulous second thoughts, second-guessing the appropriateness of such a grand, unquestioning blessing of this obviously sinful man.

Reassurance came to us when we turned to Jesus' parable of the prodigal son. We saw there the unconditionally open arms of the waiting Father. Asking nothing, requiring no promises, laying down no rules for reentry, he responds with joy to nothing more than the face turned homeward as the prodigal son walks back into the Father's territory. The disapproving elder son in Jesus' story parallels the second thoughts we had. Incredulity screamed out to get some commitment, a promise, a clue. Don't just give it to him; make some rules; extract some sorrow; set up a tentative agreement first.

But finally we returned to embrace the original thrill of "Amazing Grace," the excitement of this pastoral event, and to relish the satisfaction of having immersed, showered, and flooded this dying man with God's unconditional love. Our group was ecstatic that they had ushered into the presence of the Lord one of his dear children. And we heard the angels singing joyfully.

Reflections

1. *"They turn God's gift into a deal: 'You give that, and God returns with this.'"* Do you remember ever having this expectation? Would you say that most Christians feel this way, or that most understand the true nature of God's gift?

2. *"The seminarians showered the dying man with God's love in every way they could think of."* Describe your reaction and thoughts about 'a banquet in West Hollywood'.

3. *"The seminarians began to wonder if they should have first obtained more information about the dying man."* Do you agree they should have done so? If so, why?

4. *"Reassurance came to us when we turned to Jesus' parable of the prodigal son."* How is the story similar to that of the prodigal son? How is it different?

5. *"Our group was ecstatic that they had ushered into the presence of the Lord one of his dear children."* How would you have felt to be called upon as one of the seminarians who made the visit?

6. *"Love is not a feeling"* If love is not a feeling, what is it? Do you think the seminarians acted out of love, or duty?

7. *"The man was dying of AIDS."* Does the awareness that a person has AIDS affect your view of him/her as a child of God? How would you carry out loving care to a man with that sickness?

Chapter 14

If Jesus Were
My Teacher

If Jesus were my teacher, he would know me. I'm sure of that.

He'd know my name and how old I am and when my birthday is.

He'd know what I like and what I dislike—my hobbies, my habits, my hang-ups.

And that's a wonderful thing—to be known by someone.

It's a rare and wonderful thing to be really known!

Not only would Jesus know me, but he would notice me.

He'd notice my new haircut and my shoes, my missing teeth and bandaged fingers, my trembling chin and the tear streaks on my face.

And he would let me know very clearly that he noticed.

I'd know that he noticed.

He would hear me, too. Really hear me.

He would be

more concerned with what I mean than with what I say,

more concerned with what I'm thinking than with the accuracy of my words.

He would understand why I said what I did.

It would make sense to him, and I'd never feel wrong.

He'd always be affirming me even when I was mistaken;

he'd know the way I was thinking and what I was thinking about.

If Jesus were my teacher, he would value me.

I would be more important than anything— assignments, songs, even the furniture.

He would pay as much attention to what I feel as to what I think.
Clearly and unmistakably he would let me know

that he knew what I was feeling and that he cared!
When my friend moved away, he'd say to me, "It hurts to lose a friend."
And I'd realize that the lousy, empty feeling in my stomach was loneliness.

Knowing that, I would feel a little better,

and some of that empty feeling would go away when I sensed that he was feeling it with me.
For he would reach inside me and carefully draw out my grief—

grief I didn't even know was there—and he'd make it better.

And when I came to class one day,

bouncing with joy and excitement over the birth of my baby sister,

he'd set aside the lesson as we celebrated together all that it means to be a brother or sister.
We'd celebrate God's gift of life

and the excitement and wonder this event had brought.
Then we'd get back to work.

In a few short minutes, we'd learn the lesson twice as fast, twice as well.

Yes, he'd know me, notice me, hear me, value me, pay attention to me and to what I feel.
But also, and this is just a little different, he'd listen to me.
When others rushed in excited and chattering, and I'd stop to say, "My grandma died last night,"

he would hear and care, not absently remark, "That's nice; now take your seat."
He'd kneel beside me and put his arms around me,

healing me in seconds, faster than I ever knew was possible.
And we would talk about it with the others, everything else suddenly
unimportant.

He'd be unafraid to talk of death,
  willing to speak of it honestly without smoothing it over,
    without making it nice when it really isn't.
And, wonder of wonders, there would even be tears in his eyes!

Another thing he would do, I'm sure,
  is entrust me with his feelings, too, sharing from his life.
  His joys, excitement, hurts, fears, and disappointments
    would be appropriately presented as gifts from him to me.
And from this mutuality would develop a relationship I could never forget.
  For I was allowed into his life, and I knew him as a person, not just a
  teacher—one so like me, yet so different.
  He is so like me and still so different that I aspire to be like him—
    far more than if he merely came from on high
    and taught me what was right and true.

Oh, yes! He would respect me—
  already at age six or eight, ten, twelve, or fourteen!
Strange, bizarre, or seemingly heretical as my growing mind might be,
  he'd never say, "You don't really think that way, do you?"
    or, "You'll change your mind when you're older."
Knowing the saving, satisfying, nourishing power of respect, he would never
be worried or threatened by my thinking.

Accepting my unacceptable ideas, he'd win me to himself forever,
  and my heart would tell my mind to wander less and follow him.
He'd treat me in a way that honored my relationship with God.
I'd never get the feeling from him that big people are closer to God than
kids.

And you know what else?
You might think this silly, but if Jesus were my teacher,

I'd like him because he would touch me.

His hands would hold mine.

With his arms around me, he'd run his fingers through my hair,

and he'd squeeze my arm or pat my cheek from time to time.

And when all else through passing time had faded,

I believe that more than anything else I'd remember his touch, indelibly present where it had been.

I'd like Jesus for my teacher because he would have ideas about me, and they wouldn't be based on what my brother is like

or how excellent my sister is

or who my parents happen to be.

He'd treat me like I was just me,

created out of a special mold from which no one else was cast,

and it was an excellent one.

Despite all my differences, blemishes, weaknesses, and shortcomings,

he would treat me as just me, expecting good from me.

And I would become what he expected!

With Jesus as my teacher,

I'd even think he grew a little from knowing me.

I'd learn that I had something to contribute—

even though I was only seven or nine or twelve—

that I was a kind of teacher, too.

He'd show that I had experiences, insights, perceptions, and emotions he was fascinated with, thoughts he was intrigued by.

Oh, he'd also plan his lesson well, keep order, make sure we learned our work and maintained an attractive classroom.

He'd be at times frighteningly stern and discipline us, too—

the things an ordinary teacher does. But I'd never forget him.

I'd never stop growing in love for him and what he was

because of all those special things he had been to me.

And about those extraordinary qualities,

I'd come to see that, as he taught, I could be that way, too!

Reflections

1. *"If Jesus were my teacher..."* What or who does this title make you think about?

2. *"Not only would Jesus know me, but he would notice me."* To what level of detail do you think Jesus concerns himself about you? How do you feel about these words that we sing: "Jesus loves me, this I know."

3. *"He would understand why I said what I did."* Can you think of someone you are close to who truly understands why you do and say what do?

4. *"But also, and this is just a little different, he'd listen to me."* Do people listen to you? Do they really hear what you are saying? Describe your thoughts about the attentiveness of people to you when you speak.

5. *"Another thing he would do, I'm sure, is entrust me with his feelings, too"* How willing and patient are you to hear other people tell you what is on their heart and mind?

6. *"And I would become what he expected!"* What could help you be more like Jesus? Name one immediate change you can make in order to be more like Jesus.